Walking
THE ROYAL
CANAL

HISTORY AND LOCAL HISTORY

Peter Clarke

5 walks from Dublin to Maynooth, Co. Kildare,
along the Royal Canal.

GW00417785

ISBN 978-0-9929233-0-3

Email: canalwalks@eircom.net

Maps : Dr. Matthew Stout

Photography : Peter Clarke, Damien Clarke, Noel Spain, and Cabra for Youth Ltd.

The mural on page 4 was painted by a group of young people from Cabra aged between 10 and 12

Design and Layout: Artwerk Ltd. Dublin

Published by: Canalwalks in association with the Royal Canal Amenity Group Ltd.

Printed by: Brunswick Press Ltd. Dublin

Contents

DEDICATION

To
Catherine, our granddaughters, Kitty and Hannah

SPECIAL THANKS TO:
Frank Murphy for all his help and advice
Fergus Flanagan for editing the Guide.

My daughter Eleanor for accompanying me on many of these walks

My fellow members of RCAG and IWAI for all their help over the years.

The staff of OPW and Waterways Ireland, in particular John McKeown. They worked tirelessly to restore the canal for us all to enjoy.

Introduction

The Royal Canal

The Royal Canal links the River Liffey on the north side of Dublin to the River Shannon at Clondra in Co. Longford. The main line is 90.5 miles (145.7km) long with 46 locks (10 of these are double locks) and a sea-lock where the canal joins the River Liffey. On its journey from the Liffey in Dublin to the Shannon in Co. Longford it passes through the counties of Kildare, Meath, and Westmeath. In Co. Longford a 5.2 mile (8.4km) branch into the town of Longford is a dry section of canal. It is hoped that it will be restored in the not too distant future. In Dublin a 0.75 mile (1.2 km) section from just below Cross Guns Bridge to Broadstone in Phibsbrough was filled in, and although now considered a branch line, it was originally part of the main line when the canal first opened.

The main water supply for the canal is Lough Owel, entering on the north side of Mullingar in Co. Westmeath. The summit level is 324 (98.8m) above sea level and starts at the 25th Lock and continues for 15 miles to the 26th Lock at Coolnahay, which is six miles beyond the town of Mullingar.

The Royal Canal Company was formed in 1789 by a group of wealthy business men and politicians. It was in response to the Irish Parliament's decision to make finance available to those intending to build canals, make rivers navigable or to improve ports and harbours around Ireland.

The company proposed to build a canal system, much more extensive than the canal we have today. The original intention was for a canal 190 miles (305.7 km) long with 85 locks, 85 bridges and 75 aqueducts at a cost £197,098. One hundred and eighty eight subscribers invested £134,000 in the new company. The largest sum invested was £2,000 and smallest £100. The Irish Parliament provided an additional £66,000 or approximately one third of the cost of building the project.

To enable them to avail of the funding, the company had to lodge a map of the proposed route, and an estimate of all costs involved in building the canal. A Parliamentary committee of the Irish House of Commons was appointed to examine the proposal, to ensure that all relevant documents were received and, most importantly, to establish the viability of the project. After examining the documents the committee reported back to the House of Commons that all was in order. The sum of £66,000 was then granted to help finance the new canal. It is little wonder that the whole process went so smoothly, as the majority of this committee were directors of this new Royal Canal Company.

Like the Grand Canal, the Royal Canal was one of the most capital-intensive engineering projects to be undertaken in Ireland at the end of the eighteenth century and the beginning of the nineteenth century. Construction began in 1790, and as could be expected, many problems were encountered throughout its construction. By 1794, with only fifteen miles of canal under construction, the entire capital of the company had been absorbed and it was in effect bankrupt. Although this was a major engineering project, the Royal Canal Company only employed a part-time engineer to supervise the work in the early days of construction. As a result of there being little or no supervision as the work proceeded, some of the bridges collapsed killing and injuring work men. Many of the locks had to be rebuilt due to bad workmanship and the poor quality of the materials used in their construction. Added to these problems the proposed route was often changed to enable the canal pass through, or close to, property owned by some of the directors. In Co. Kildare the canal was to pass north of Maynooth; the Duke of Leinster however had the route changed so that it would pass his estate at Carton and on through the town.

By 1809 the canal was completed as far as Coolnahay, six miles past Mullingar in Co. Westmeath. At that stage the company was heavily in debt and unable to complete the rest of the line to the River Shannon. The government had no option but to intervene, and it was decided to dissolve the company in 1813, and complete the canal, using public funding. The canal was completed to Richmond Harbour in Clondra, Co. Longford in 1817 and the following year The New Royal Canal Company was formed, with a government-appointed board to oversee its affairs. The Royal Canal was never a commercial success; it took twenty-eight years to build at a cost of £1.5 million. By mid 1800s rail had begun to make its mark in Ireland and so in 1845 the Midland Great Western Railway Company purchased the canal for £318,860, with a view to building the line in the bed of the canal. However, the Act that allowed the railway company to purchase the canal, also stated that as a condition the canal must always remain a separate transport system. There are a number of books written on this canals history, among them my own, Peter Clarke, *The Royal Canal, The Complete Story* and Ruth Delany's *Ireland's Royal Canal*, if you want to explore the full history written on this Canal.

Over the past twenty-five years, I have lectured and written on the history of the Royal Canal. I have also led a variety of groups on canal walks, organised by the Royal Canal Amenity Group, outlining both canal and local history. The walks described in this guide will satisfy either the experienced long- distance walker or those who just want a stroll on one of the shorter sections of the canal. Whether you are an experienced walker or Sunday stroller, the freedom of the towpath is there for you to enjoy, as you step back in time to when life was lived at a slower pace and follow in the steps of the horse-drawn barges.

A little advice before you set off

Be careful, while water is beautiful to look at and walk beside, it can also be dangerous, particularly if you are on your own. Take care when you are close to the water's edge, and at the lock chambers in particular, they are deep and it could be difficult to climb out if you fall in!

Wear comfortable walking shoes and have weatherproof clothing if you are going to walk a long distance. Bring a snack and a flask if you are heading off for the day. Tell someone where you are going and don't forget to charge up your mobile phone before you set off.

Observe and enjoy the wildlife but please don't disturb them. The gates, fences and canal fittings are important to us all, so don't damage them and leave as you found them. Respect this wonderful amenity; bring your litter home with you and only leave your footprint when you head home.

The towpath along the canal is designated **The Royal Canal Way** and is there for all of us to enjoy. The walks described in this guide are safe for all ages, but special care should be taken where young children are involved. Commonsense standards of both water safety and road safety should be observed at all times.

The towpath along the Canal from the Liffey to the Shannon is a mixture of grass, gravel and tarmac and it is possible to walk its full length. For walking and other activities on the Royal Canal contact

Waterways Ireland at info@waterwaysireland.org.

Mural at the 5th lock.

Royal Canal Amenity Group

A public meeting in Maynooth was organised by An Taisce, in 1970, in response to a plan to close the canal and replace with a roadway. It was stated that there was no reason why the canal could not be saved, apart from the cost. It was not until 1974 that positive steps were taken towards restoration. In the *Inland Waterways News* Dr. Ian Bath suggested that a group or federation be formed to spearhead the protection and development of the canal. This was supported by Ruth Delany, chairperson of the Dublin Branch of the Inland Waterways Association of Ireland. In April 1974 Ian founded the Royal Canal Amenity Group (RCAG) with the aim of highlighting the amenity potential of a restored canal. Over the summer months of 1974, work parties operated in the evening and at weekends clearing the channel and towpath between Castleknock and Blanchardstown. Support for the group grew throughout 1974-75 and soon a seven and a half mile section of the canal was restored to full depth. Over the years the movement expanded and branches were formed in towns and villages along the route of the canal. In 1986 the ownership was transferred from CIE to OPW (Waterways Ireland). Working together the canal was fully restored from the Liffey to the Shannon in 2011. RCAG no longer run work parties on the canal, but work in close collaboration with Waterways Ireland and its staff, helping to promote the canal and its activates.

For further information see www.royalcanal.net

The Inland Waterways Association of Ireland

The Inland Waterways Association of Ireland was founded in 1954 to campaign for the conservation and development of our inland waterways. It's a voluntary body that promotes the maintenance, protection, restoration and improvement of all our inland waterways. For further information see *iwai.ie*.

WALK 1

Newcomen Bridge, North Strand
To
Cross Guns Bridge, Phibsborough

Distance	1.2 miles (2.1km)
Terrain	Tarmac surface all the way

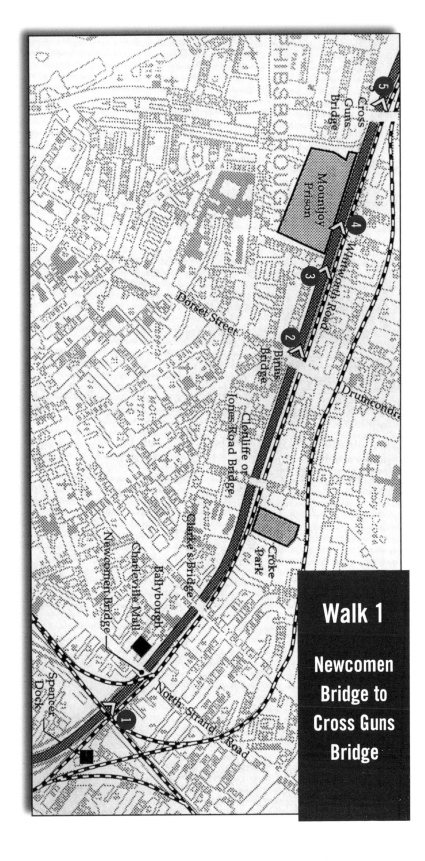

Walk 1

Newcomen
Bridge to
Cross Guns
Bridge

If you are only starting to explore the canal this is the ideal walk to begin with. The canal rises out of the city by a series of locks and levels, just like the steps on a flight of stairs, passing under old granite stone bridges, which are a feature of the canal all the way to the River Shannon. Come hail, rain or shine the tarmac towpath, which accompanies you all the way, makes this an easy and most enjoyable walk.

Starting at Newcomen Bridge on the North Strand, at Charleville Mall Library, the towpath continues on the south bank of the canal to Clarke's Bridge and on past Croke Park, the headquarters of the GAA. The next bridge is Jones's Road Bridge (Clonliffe Bridge) and from here it continues to Binns Bridge Drumcondra, on the main Dublin to Belfast road, after which it changes to the north bank of the canal. Here you will encounter the seated sculpture of one of our most famous authors and playwrights, Brendan Behan. He sits sprawled on his seat, pondering the waters of the canal and the nearby Mountjoy Jail. From here to Cross Gun's Bridge on the Phibsborough Road, the towpath is laid out as a linear park, and is provided with seating, set along the well maintained grass margins. This section of the canal has four locks along its length, 2nd, 3rd, 4th and 5th. As you reach the 4th lock you get a splendid view back over the canal and the north city, towards Croke Park and the red and white chimneys of Ringsend Power Station.

History

Spencer Dock

From Newcomen Bridge back towards the River Liffey is known as Spencer Dock, named after Earl Spencer who performed the opening ceremony. Initially this section was built wider than the rest of the canal, as it was to accommodate a floating dock. However, this was abandoned soon after work commenced on the project in 1793. The Midland Great Western Railway Company, who bought the Royal Canal Company in 1845, extended the wharfage accommodation along this section in 1854 and railway facilities were provided down to the river. Again, in 1873 further alterations were carried out, increasing the quay frontage and the installation of a Sea Lock at the river, allowing small sea vessels to enter the dock, where they could connect directly with the railway.

Newcomen Bridge and the 1st Lock

Newcomen Bridge, like the majority of the bridges on this section is named after Canal Company directors, and in many cases these locations had an association with the particular director. William Gleadowe of Killester was said to be an ambitious and unscrupulous social climber, a young man who was eager to make his fortune in a hurry. To ensure his future and fulfill his ambitions, he married Charlotte Newcomen, a young lady of considerable means from Carriglas, Co. Longford, in 1773, and changed his name to Newcomen. Having secured a wife and taken her name and her wealth he then went into the banking business, opening a bank in Mary's Abbey off Capel Street in the city centre. Due to his wife's influence he gained a seat in the Irish Parliament and earned himself a Privy Councillorship and a Baronetcy. The banking business went well for Sir William, and he soon

The 1st Lock, Newcomen Bridge North Strand.

moved to a larger and more imposing headquarters in Castle Street, off Dame Street, close to Dublin Castle. When the Canal Company was formed in 1789, he became a director and its first treasurer. Shortly after the work commenced, the company met with severe financial difficulties, but help was at hand when Newcomen and his bank came to the rescue with a loan to help carry on the work. However, the price was very high indeed, for this noble action Newcomen charged 30% interest on the loan. This was described by some of his fellow directors at the time as "most exorbitant and illegal profit". Sir William died in 1807 never seeing the completed canal.

During the construction of Newcomen Bridge, which collapsed because of poor workmanship, two workmen unfortunately lost their lives. Many years later, tragedy was to strike close to the same spot, when in May 1941, German bombs fell on the North Strand beside this bridge. 41 people were killed, many more were injured and hundreds lost their homes.

Ballybough

Clarke's Bridge on the Ballybough Road, is a fine example of an original canal bridge. Built with granite stone, it is named after another canal director, Edward Clarke. The nearby Tolka River, which passes through Ballybough, marked the southern boundary of the ancient territory of Fingal. The first bridge over the Tolka was built for the convenience of those travelling to and from maritime Fingal, over 600 years ago. Ballybough is a thriving community, its mixture of new and old housing adding to its charm. However in the 17th and 18th century the area was known as Mud Island. This settlement of mud- cabins was home to the city highwaymen and smugglers. Mud Island had its own king, Art Granger, in the 18th century. It is claimed that his ghost haunted the area around the canal.

Croke Park

Croke Park is situated between Clarke's Bridge and Jones's Road Bridge (Clonliffe Bridge). The famous Canal End Stand dominates this section of canal. The site has a long association with sport. In the 1870's it was the *City and Suburban Race*

Course but was generally referred to as *Jones's Road Sports Ground.* It failed as a race course and was then hired out for various sporting activities including athletics, boxing and ladies football. The Gaelic Athletic Association (GAA) used the grounds frequently for hurling and football matches. The All Ireland finals were held here in 1896. Originally the site contained 14 acres, but the Jesuit Community at Belvedere College bought 4 acres and in 1913 the GAA bought the remaining 10 acres for £3,500. In recent years the College sold back the 4 acres to the Association. To-day it is the principal ground and administrative headquarters of the Association and one of the largest and best-equipped sports stadium in Europe.

The Canal End, Croke Park.

Binns Bridge (Drumcondra)

The Dublin to Belfast road crosses the canal at Binns Bridge. John Binns was the man who founded the Royal Canal Company in 1789. He and his partner William Cope were wholesale silk merchants in Shaw Street, Dublin; both were also directors of the Grand Canal Company. Binns was also a politician, commonly known as Long John Binns or to his enemies (of which there were many), as the *devils darning needle*. He represented the weavers on Dublin City Common Council. When the Royal Canal Company was formed it got considerable help from the Irish Parliament, who assumed that all the documents supplied by the Company, such as the estimates for the work and the survey of the proposed route were genuine. It was not until 1796, six years after work began, that it was discovered that these documents were in effect forged. No survey had ever taken place on the line of the proposed canal. Binns himself concocted the estimate, using information from work carried out on the Grand Canal. The cost of building the canal, (including the locks, aqueducts and bridges), were guessed at, making it impossible for the project to succeed. Binns lived close to this bridge at 59 Dorset Street. He died before the canal was completed.

Brendan Behan

Mountjoy Prison

From Binns Bridge to the next bridge, the towpath is wide with a good tarmac surface. It is along this particular bank of canal that "the auld triangle went jingle jangle". Mountjoy Prison or *"The Joy,"* as it is more affectionately known, was opened for business in 1850. Mountjoy is named after Luke Gardiner, Lord Mountjoy. Gardiner's grandfather also called Luke was the largest land owner and property developer on the north side of Dublin. He was responsible for developing Sackville Street (O'Connell Street) and Henrietta Street, Dublin's most important Georgian street. The young Luke made his mark on our fair city by building Mountjoy Square, Gardiner and Blessington Streets. However, his greatest development plan only managed to make it to the drawing stage. His Royal Circus development was to be built where the Mater Hospital and the Prison now stand. This development consisted of several avenues of Georgians houses, leading to an elliptical shaped centre-piece of splendid Georgian mansions. They were to resemble Castletown House in Co. Kildare and the houses of Bath in England. One of the avenues was to

The 4th lock

be named Cowley Place and was to run directly to the 4th lock on the canal, allowing the new transport system to link townhouse and country estate. Unfortunately, Luke Gardiner was killed at the battle of New Ross in Wexford in the 1798 Rebellion, and with him died the dream of the Royal Circus.

Looking north across the railway track, you can see the headquarters of the National Council of the Blind in Ireland (NCBI) on Whitworth Road. The small gated avenue alongside it leads to the rear of the building and the burial ground for Saint George's Church in nearby Temple Street. This graveyard was donated to the church by Luke Gardiner.

The church was the masterpiece of the architect Francis Johnston. It stands 200 feet high with a five-storey clock tower and spire. He also designed amongst other buildings in the city, the General Post Office in O'Connell Street. Francis Johnston died in 1829 and is buried in the graveyard.

Cross Guns Bridge and the 5th Lock

We end this part of our journey at Cross Guns Bridge on the Phibsborough Road. The Cross Guns is named from an inn which was situated a little to the north of here at Hart's Corner. John Rocque's 1761 map of Dublin shows that a hamlet had developed around this spot. But by 1816 the area had developed and was incorporated into the greater Glasnevin area. Through time the location was lost and to-day all that remains is the name associated with the canal-bridge.

Phibsborough is only a short distance away, where there are a variety of shops and places to eat and also bus services to the city.

Wildlife at Phibsborough

WALK 2

The Broadstone Branch
Cross Guns Bridge
To
Broadstone (Phibsborough)

Droichead Blaquiere
BLAQUIERE BRIDGE
D.C.C. PARK SERVICES

Distance	1.6 miles (3km)
Terrain	Footpath all the way

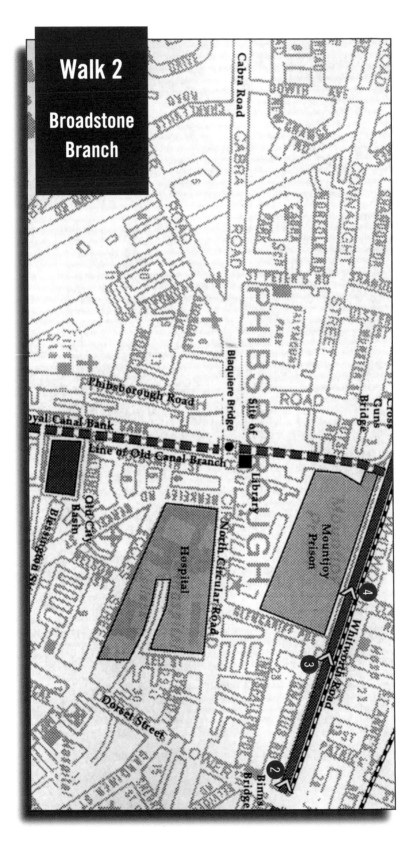

Walk 2

Broadstone Branch

This section of the canal is commonly known as "the branch." However, when the canal was first built, this was the main line, and the section from Cross Guns Bridge (Westmoreland Bridge), to the River Liffey was considered a spur by the Royal Canal Company.

You can start this walk at Binns Bridge on the south bank of the canal or from Cross Guns Bridge on Phibsborough Road. From Binns Bridge you continue along the outer wall of Mountjoy Prison. From Cross Guns Bridge continue down the slip road to Royal Canal Villas.

Although the canal water no longer flows along this section, it still makes for a pleasant walk along the linear park, and down to the old North City Basin. Half way down this section is Phibsborough Library, built in 1934, seven years after the canal was filled in. At the library cross the North Circular Road (where the canal passed under Blaquiere Bridge) and continue on the tree lined park down to the City Basin. The entrance to the Basin is through the black door in high stone wall a short distance along the path. This almost forgotten secret garden, in the heart of Dublin City, is home to a variety of wild life, including Mallard, Tufted duck, Cormorants and Herons. The main entrance to the Basin is at the top of Blessington Street a mere half mile from O'Connell Street. Leaving the basin, and returning to the park, turn left past the children's playground and continue a short distance to

Royal Canal Bank Phibsborough

Broadstone. The two renovated houses on the right, backing on to the new student's accommodation, was at one time the Royal Canal ticket office. Here intending passengers bought their tickets for the journey westwards along the canal. As you enter out into Broadstone two elegant buildings capture the skyline. To the left is the King's Inns and to the right is the old Broadstone Railway Station where the old canal harbour and hotel were once part of a busy canal scene. There is a footpath for the entire route and comfortable walking shoes are all that are required. Care should be taken when crossing main roads, such as North Circular Road and the Phibsborough Road.

From here you can return back along the Phibsborough Road through Phibsborough with its shops, restaurants and other facilities, to Cross Guns Bridge and the 5th Lock, where this walk started. On the other hand you can explore the King's Inns and then go down to the city-centre through historic Henrietta Street, one of Ireland's most important Georgian streets.

The History

Building the Canal

Just below Cross Guns Bridge work started on building the canal in May 1790. 2,000 men were employed as "navvies" to dig the canal with picks and shovels. Working in gangs of 140, spread out along the route, eastwards towards the Liffey, westwards towards Ashtown and in the direction of Broadstone. It was a long working-day from dawn to dusk and the wages of 10 pence per day was hard earned. The navvies or navigators were rough, tough men; many of them lived in makeshift huts along the canal bank. They cooked their meagre rations of oatmeal porridge and bread, which was the staple diet, on open fires. While the majority of the men were Irish, some travelled from England to work on the canal. It was common for contests to occur between them to see who could dig a length of canal in the shortest time. It was not unusual for a bet to be placed on the event and in many instances the Irish won.

Work started at dawn and continued until the daylight faded. Six days was the normal working week, but in fine

weather it was extended to seven. The working conditions were terrible: hour after hour, day after day, mile after mile they dug, loading the heavy, wet earth into timber barrows and dragging them up the ten feet from the bottom of the canal cutting, to the top of the bank. There was little comfort for the canal navvies. Those who could return to their homes did so at the end of an exhausting day's work. The less fortunate, most likely, found their way to the nearest inn where they spent their pennies trying to forget the drudgery of the day.

Sir John de Blaquiere (The King's Cowman)

The bridge on the North Circular Road was named after Sir John de Blaquiere KP who lived close to the canal at the 4th Lock. Blaquiere, also a director of the Royal Canal Company was more commonly known as "The King's Cowman" and was at one time Chief Secretary of State in Ireland from 1772 until 1777. In 1794 he took up the position as Bailiff of the Phoenix Park. This entitled him to a salary of £9 per year and a small six roomed lodge to live in. A wealthy and influential man, Blaquiere was also a Member of Parliament and represented the Borough of Charleville in Co. Tipperary and also Enniskillen and Carlingford. Not content with his accommodation in the park, he illegally walled off 35 acres surrounding the lodge. Outraged by this, James Napper Tandy, a noted nationalist, took Blaquiere to court in 1795. However, Napper Tandy had very little chance of winning the case. The three judges were friends of Blaquiere and the jury was hand picked. Blaquiere was awarded £8,000 compensation, which he put to good use. He built himself a splendid new residence on the site of the old lodge (now the residence of the American Ambassador). He later succeeded in having his salary as a bailiff increased to £50 per year and unlimited grazing for his stock in the Park. Little else is known of John Blaquiere: it is said that he was the 5th son of a Swiss emigrant who had settled in London. However, it is also stated "that his source is like that of the Nile, it has never been discovered with certainty"

The Old City Basin

In 1808 an agreement was reached between the Royal Canal Company and Dublin Corporation for a water supply from the canal, to feed the expanding north side of Dublin. The Basin which covers approximately 1.75 acres was completed in 1809 to the design of the renowned Scottish engineer John Rennie. To mark its opening on the 25th of October and the Golden Jubilee of King George III, it was named *The Royal George Reservoir*, a name seldom used to-day. The Basin has a capacity of almost five million gallons of water, is 410 feet (125 metres) long and 190 feet (58 metres) wide and has an average depth of eight feet (2.4 metres). Much of the earth excavated from the Basin was used to help raise the level of Upper Dominick Street, which was under construction at that time, and more was used to build-up the embankment at Broadstone Harbour, the terminus of the canal.

The Basin served the north side of Dublin for nearly 60 years, including the nearby Mater Hospital when it was first opened in 1862. From time to time there were many complaints about the quality of the water provided, and these complaints were probably justified. The locals used the canal to wash clothes, and neighbourhood dogs found it a delightful spot for their daily paddle. Its primitive filter system of a wire mesh and gravel bank across its centre, was of little use. The cattle boats using the canal frequently unloaded the residue of their cargo into the nearby canal harbour at Broadstone.

Old City Basin

In 1868 the city got its water supply from the new Vartry Water Works and so the Basin became redundant. Over the years various proposals were put forward as to what it could be used for, including a swimming pool, but little interest was shown from local people and so the ideas were dropped. Up until 1967 it continued to supply local industry with up to half a million gallons of water per day. After the Broadstone section of canal closed, the supply was taken from the 8th Lock at Cabra. Between 1993 and 1994 Dublin Corporation carried out extensive renovations to the Basin and when the work was completed it was discovered that the supply pipe from the canal had deteriorated beyond repair, it was then decided to fill the Basin from the main's water supply. This almost forgotten secret garden in the heart of Dublin City, is home to a variety of wild life including mallard, tufted duck, cormorants and herons. The main entrance to the basin is at the top of Blessington Street.

Broadstone

Further along the park, past the rear of the new student accommodation building, and towards Broadstone two elegant buildings capture the skyline. To the left is the King's Inns and to the right is the old Broadstone Railway Station. The King's Inns was designed by the architect James Gandon in 1785; he also designed other iconic buildings in the city such as the Custom House and the Four Courts. The King's Inns was Gandon's last commission before retiring, passing the work on to his pupil, Henry Aaron Baker who completed the project. James Gandon died at his home at Cannonbrook in Lucan Co. Dublin in 1823 and is buried in the Church of Ireland Cemetery, Drumcondra with his good friend Capt. Francis Grose. The name Broadstone comes from the Norse Bradog-Steyn or flat stone that crossed the River Bradoge here at Broadstone.The Bradoge River, now culverted, flows down through Cabra, the Kings Inn and Bolton Street on its way to the River Liffey.

When the canal barges travelled along this section of canal they crossed over the Phibsborough Road to the canal habour via a large stone aqueduct, designed by the architects, Miller and Roddy. The aqueduct was named in honour of John Foster, the last speaker of the Irish House of Commons. It was a fine example of early 19th century engineering; its main

The King's Inns

Broadstone Railway Station

arch had a span of 30 feet with two smaller arches on either side, allowing those travelling on foot to pass underneath. The aqueduct was demolished in 1951 to facilitate the widening of Phibsborough Road.

This was a busy place in the early 1800s. Boats arrived daily, with cargoes of cattle, pigs, turf and a variety of agricultural produce from the midlands, and returned home laden with coal, barrels of porter and tea etc.

Passengers were also part of the busy scene as they arrived and departed to various destinations along the length of the canal. The Royal Canal Company purchased this site and an adjoining house and garden in 1789 for the sum of £1500. Included with this purchase was an acre of land in Glasnevin. Later this was bought by the Botanic Gardens and is now commonly known as the Rose Garden. The Canal Company later converted the house to a hotel, but the venture failed and it was closed in 1812. Although the railway company built a new house on the site, part of the old house remains in use at No. 1 Phibsborough Road.

In 1845 the Midland Great Western Railway Company bought the canal and built a railway track parallel to it from Dublin to Mullingar in Co. Westmeath. To service the new transport system a new terminus was needed. The Railway Company commissioned the renowned railway architect John

Skipton Mulvany to design the new station on the site of the old canal habour at Broadstone. Construction of this magnificent Neo-Egyptian style granite building began in 1846 and was completed to Mulvany's design in 1850 by the builder Gilbert Cockburn and Sons. The railway was an instant success; it could carry a lot more goods and passengers in a much faster time. The Canal Company had commenced its passenger service from here to Kilcock in Co. Kildare in December 1796, and the last passenger boat left the harbour on the 2nd of October 1848, for the eight hour journey to Mullingar. In 1861 extensive alterations were made to the station, when it was extended with the erection of a colonnade on the eastern side of the station. Commercial canal traffic continued to use the canal until 1879 when the harbour was filled in.

From here you can return back along the Phibsborough Road through Phibsborough, with its shops, restaurants and other facilities to Cross Guns Bridge and the 5th Lock, where this walk started. On the other hand, you can explore the King's Inns and then go on down to the city-centre through historic Henrietta Street, one of Ireland's most important Georgian streets.

No 1 Phibsborough Road

<u>WALK 3</u>

Cross Guns Bridge (5th Lock) Phibsborough
To
The 12th Lock Blanchardstown

Distance	4.2 miles (6.7km)
Terrain	Hard surface all the way

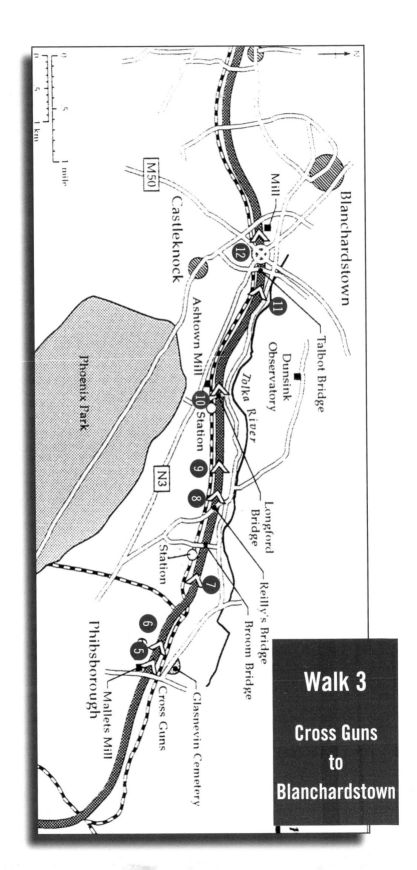

Walk 3

Cross Guns
to
Blanchardstown

The tow-path from the 5th Lock at Cross Guns Bridge to Broome Bridge has a hard tarmac surface and is also used by cars as far as the Coke Oven Cottages. At the 6th Lock the path rises sharply, giving a splendid view over Glasnevin Cemetery and the north side of the City. Passing the houses on Shandon Park and the Coke Oven Cottages, the canal passes the rear of Batchelor's food processing plant in Cabra on the left-hand side. Passing under the bridge of the Sligo Railway line, by a pedestrian underpass to the 7th Lock, you will see the old water tower of Liffey Junction Railway Station, closed to passengers in 1926. Broome Bridge is now in sight, and only a short distance from here it is possible to return to the city by train or bus.

From Broome Bridge to Reilly's Bridge the tow-path has a hard surface. Care should be taken when crossing over Reilly's Bridge between the tow-paths. The bridge is an off centre bridge and at the time of writing a new bridge is under construction. From here to Longford Bridge at Ashtown, the tow-path has a hard tarmac surface, as the canal skirts the new housing development of Scribblestown. In recent years the area around Ashtown and the canal has been developed with shops and pubs serving food beside the newly reopened railway station. From here to the 12th Lock at Blanchardstown,

the towpath is suitable for walking and cycling and is one of the most picturesque sections of the canal. The peace and tranquility broken only by the passing trains on the adjacent rail line. This walk ends at the 12th Lock on the outskirts of the major suburb of Blanchardstown. Here all services are provided for, including an excellent bus service returning to the city centre via the Navan Road, Phibsborough or Stoneybatter. The 12th Lock Marina and the Twelfth Lock Hotel complex are situated just beyond Longford Bridge. This hotel won the best new hotel in Ireland award at the National Hospitality Awards in 2004, and the best presented hotel and surroundings in 2004 and 2005. Also included in the complex is the Twelfth Lock Bar and Dam Square Bistro. A short distance along the tow-path is Castleknock Railway Station from where you can return to the city by commuter train.

The History

Cross Guns Bridge (Westmoreland Bridge and the 5th Lock)

It was expected that the canal would bring prosperity, trade and industry to the small towns along the routes. However, this only happened in a very limited way and the majority of the canal-side industries only developed in Dublin City and County areas. Between Cross Guns Bridge and Blanchardstown only four industries developed. Two of these were later converted to apartments, one is unoccupied and the other was demolished after it went on fire. An apartment block was built on the site.

Westmoreland Lock was the first lock to be built on the canal; the Royal Canal Company considered this to be the 1st lock and from here to the Liffey was to be the canal branch. What is now called the branch to Broadstone was the main line in the early years. The foundation stone for the lock was laid on Thursday 12th November 1790 by John Fane, Earl of Westmoreland. The ceremony attracted such a large crowd that it was necessary for the military to keep control. The Earl was presented with an inscribed silver trowel to mark the occasion, and he in turn, very generously, presented twenty guineas to Richard Evans, the part-time engineer, to be

View from the 6th Lock Phibsborough

distributed among the workmen. Like all the lock chambers on the canal it is built of dressed limestone. The original gates were made from Irish Oak and cost £200 per set for the small gates and £300 for the deep gates, including fitting. Both the lock and the bridge were completed in May 1791 at a cost of £1846-9s-4d. The original hump-backed bridge was restructured and widened in 1912 and levelled in mid-1920. The Brian Boru Public House is a well known landmark just beside the bridge. Although the present building dates from 1850 there was a public house on this site for over 200 years. Michael and Peter Hedigan are the third generation of the Hedigan family running the business and welcome visitors to the venue for refreshments and meals. The Brian Boru is mentioned in James Joyce's *Ulysses*. Joyce refers to the mourners as they pass by on their way to Glasnevin Cemetery.

Mallett's Mill

The large limestone building on the left bank at the 5th Lock, now converted to luxury apartments, was formerly part of Mallett's (Mill) Iron Works, locally known as *Malletts Folly*. The Royal Canal Company referred to all industrial buildings as mills. This was one of the first mills to be built on the canal. Robert and John Mallett leased this site from the Royal Canal Company in 1822, and gradually began to move their thriving engineering business from the city-centre to this canal-side location. At that time this marked the city boundary. It was here at Mallets that the railings which surround the Nassau Street side of Trinity College were made and they are still standing and in good condition to the present day. John Mallett's son, Robert was a scientist and an inventor. Born in 1810 he entered Trinity College at the age of sixteen to study Maths and science. After graduating he worked in the family business and in 1832 he was elected to the Royal Irish Academy at the age of twenty two. He was an early pioneer of seismology, which studies the power and energy unleashed by earthquakes. Today Robert Mallett is considered the father of seismology, and is credited with coining the name. In 1860 the Iron Works closed. The new owners, Murtagh Brothers, who acquired the mill and converted it to flour mill, which it remained in that capacity until it finally ceased operation in the mid 1980s.

Shandon Park Mill and the 6th Lock

There is only a very short distance between the 5th and 6th locks and it's here we meet the second of our "City Mills". This is Shandon Park Mill, originally built as a corn mill, but over the years it has served many purposes, including a log store for the nearby Railway Company from 1848 until 1885, and then as a pin and rivet factory until early 1900. In 1928 it was taken over by William Blake, who set up a factory to manufacture bread rusk for use in sausage making, and later expanded into the business of pepper and spice- grinding. The mill was badly damaged by fire in 1943, and although most of its machinery was destroyed, it was back in production in a short time. The mill was incorporated into a new housing development in 1994 when it was converted to apartments.

The dominant view from the 6th lock is of the O'Connell Monument in Glasnevin Cemetery. Originally the tower was to form part of a cluster of buildings representing early Irish Christian architecture, and was designed by the noted antiquarian George Petrie. The purpose of the development, which included a chapel and a Celtic cross, was to honour

The O'Connell Monument, Glasnevin Cemetery

Daniel O'Connell. The tower was completed in 1869 and stands at a height of just over 168 feet (51 metres) but the rest of the development was abandoned because the Tower dwarfed and distorted the scale of the other buildings.

The cemetery was opened, on a nine acre plot, in February 1832; the first person to be interred was a young boy, Michael Carey of Francis Street in Dublin's Liberties. Prior to the opening of the Cemetery at Prospect (later called Glasnevin Cemetery), Irish Catholics had no cemetery of their own in which they could bury their dead. This was due to the repressive 18th century Penal Laws which placed heavy restrictions on the public performance of any Catholic services. An incident in which a Catholic priest was reprimanded for carrying out a service at a funeral Mass, prompted Daniel O'Connell to push for the opening of a burial ground in which both Catholics and other faiths could be buried with dignity.

In the 1830's, funerals entering the cemetery were forced to pay a toll at the junction of the Finglas and Glasnevin Roads (Harts Corner). To avoid paying the toll a new road was opened directly into the graveyard from this junction, thus avoiding the turnpike. It was O'Connell who suggested the new road and so was born the phrase "that he could drive a coach and four through an Act of Parliament." The Act which established the turnpike and the coach and four was

Glasnevin Cemetery

the horse-drawn hearse on its way to the, cemetery. In the early 1850s the high walls and towers which surround the cemetery were erected. This was to prevent the stealing of the bodies from the newly opened graves by the sack-em-ups. Dublin medical schools needed a vast number of bodies to dissect and improve their medical knowledge. Dead bodies were in short supply and so a lucrative trade developed in grave robbing. An adult body could fetch as much as two pounds, and a child's body was sold by the inch! The main entrance to the cemetery was moved from Prospect Square to the Finglas Road in 1879. Today the cemetery covers an area of 124 acres, tours are organised daily and the restaurant, museum and genealogy centre are well worth visiting. A new entrance between the graveyard and the Botanic Gardens was opened in 2013 and it is hoped visitors may be able to ascend O'Connell's Tower when it is refurbished in late 2014.

Broome Bridge

Although this bridge is named after William Broome, another canal director, it has become famous because of its association with Sir William Rowan Hamilton. Hamilton was born at 36 Lower Dominick Street at midnight on August the 3rd 1805.

He was considered a child prodigy, at the age of seven he could read Hebrew and by his early teens he was proficient at thirteen other languages. However, it was as a mathematician that he is best known. While the Hamilton family was an educated family, it is thought that young William's genius was inherited from his mother, Sarah Hutton. At the age of twenty-two he was appointed Professor of Astronomy at Trinity College Dublin and in 1827 he became Astronomer Royal of Ireland at Dunsink Observatory. On Monday the 16th of October 1843, while he and his wife Helen were on their way to Dublin, where he was to preside at a Council Meeting of the Royal Irish Academy in Dawson Street, they walked along the canal towards Broome Bridge. William was preoccupied and almost unaware of Helen's presence. It was at this point that the idea of Quaternions came to him. In his excitement Hamilton rushed forward to the bridge, and carved his new found formula $I^2 = J^2 = K^2 = IJK = -1$ or the *fundamental formula for quaternion multiplication* on the stone capping. He hoped that his new discovery would revolutionise mathematical physics. Today his formula is used in a range of processes from computer graphics to space travel. He was a close friend of the poet William Wordsworth, and it is most likely that they both walked the canal on one of Wordsworth's frequent visits to Ireland.

The final years of Hamilton's life were unhappy. The deaths of his sister, Catherine, and his friend Wordsworth, led to depression and alcohol abuse and he became a recluse, and died at Dunsink on the 2nd September 1865. To-day there is a crater on the moon named after this great mathematician. There is a simple plaque on the bridge commemorating his discovery and was unveiled by a fellow mathematician, Eamon de Valera, in 1943 to mark the 100th anniversary of his discovery.

Rowan Hamilton's plaque on Broome Bridge

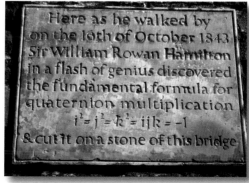

Here as he walked by
on the 16th of October 1843
Sir William Rowan Hamilton
in a flash of genius discovered
the fundamental formula for
quaternion multiplication
$i^2 = j^2 = k^2 = ijk = -1$
& cut it on a stone of this bridge

Ashtown

Just beyond Longford Bridge is Ashtown Mill, the third mill on this section of canal. Unlike the two other mills, this one was set much further back from the canal. Nevertheless it did use canal water as an energy source and some parts of the mill-race are still visible from the tow-path. The water was returned to the canal through a small arch on the city side of Longford Bridge. The 1837 ordnance survey map of the area, describes it as a linseed oil mill, but over the years it was used for many purposes, including a candle factory and a polish factory. The clock which was on the front of the mill is said to have come from Newgate Jail in Green Street in Dublin.

The 12th Lock at Blanchardstown

The 12th Lock and Talbot Bridge near Blanchardstown is the finishing point for this Walk 3. Blanchardstown Mill was the 4th mill built on the Dublin stretch of the canal. A lease was granted to Thomas Bryan for a site to build a woollen mill here at the 12th lock in 1822. When the mill went into production it employed between 80 and 100 local people. Although it has been used for a variety of purposes over the years, it only ceased production as a working factory in 1994, when a fire damaged the building and it was demolished. Some of the stone was saved and incorporated into the new apartment development built on the site.

Blanchardstown was a small village on the road between Dublin and Navan right up until the early 1970's. Today it is a busy suburb of Dublin offering all amenities and facilities, while still retaining its rural village charm. It is only a short distance away from where a full range of services are available.

Broome Bridge

WALK 4

12th Lock Blanchardstown
To
Louisa Bridge Leixlip

Distance	6.7 miles (10.7km)
Terrain	Hard surface and grass

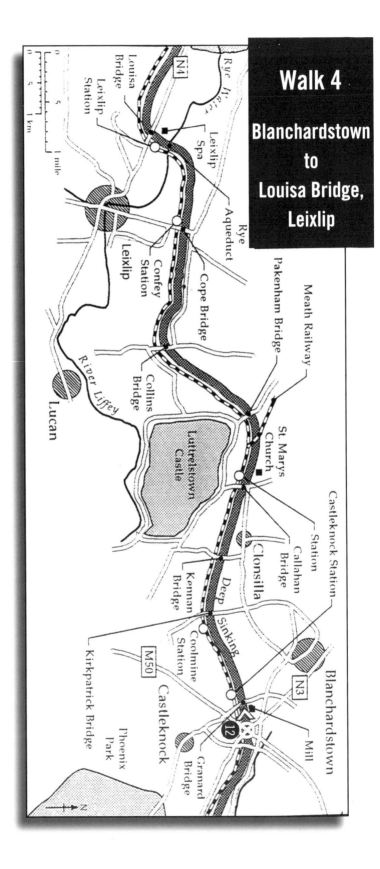

Walk 4

Blanchardstown to Louisa Bridge, Leixlip

Standing on the 12th Lock, looking back along the canal across the woods and fields of Blanchardstown, you can see the large dome of Dunsink Observatory in the distance. The 12th Lock marks the start of a 7.5 mile (12km) stretch of canal without locks, ending at the 13th Lock between Leixlip and Maynooth Co. Kildare. In the summer of 1974 the newly formed Royal Canal Amenity Group, operating in the evenings and weekends, cleared the over grown towpath from just above this lock up to Granard Bridge at Castleknock. They cleared the channel, allowing it to be used for small boats, and laid out a walking area and a nature trail. From this small beginning the group's activities spread back along the canal towards Dublin and westwards towards the River Shannon. Within a short time, branches of the group were formed in some of the towns and villages along the route, with a view to restoring the whole navigation for leisure use.

There is only a short distance between Talbot Bridge at the 12th Lock and the next bridge, Granard Bridge and Castleknock Railway Station. At many of the bridges you will see grooves cut deep into the stonework. These were formed from the wet ropes, as the horse pulled his heavy load along the waterway. It reminds us that this was not always a place of leisure, but a working canal. Granard Bridge is the start of the 1.75 mile (2.8km) Deep Sinking. From here the tow-path is narrow and rises gradually to a height of 30 feet above the surface of the water. In wet or damp weather the

Grooves cut into the bridge from the wet ropes

limestone rock which forms part of the towpath, can be very slippery. Groups should walk in a single file and extreme care should be taken.

The next bridge is Kirkpatrick Bridge, followed by Kennan Bridge at Porterstown, where the towpath changes to the right or north bank of the canal. The towpath improves from here to Callahan Bridge at Clonsilla Railway Station. At this point the canal leaves behind the housing estates of Dublin City and County and enters the open country side. The wide and grassy towpath is pleasant for walking and you soon pass under the old Dublin-Meath railway line, now reopened to Dunboyne. Pakenham Bridge at Barberstown is the next bridge, followed by Collins Bridge at Coldblow. From here it's a little over 0.5 mls (.8km) to the Royal Canal Amenity Group's leisure park, boat house and boat slip at Confey. The Boat House was built by the group to store small boats and the equipment used for the restoration work on the canal. The slipway was added at a later stage and the area behind the boat house was cleared and developed as a picnic area. A short distance further on is Confey Railway Station at Cope Bridge. You can leave the canal here and take a 15 minute walk to Leixlip where all services are available including a bus service to Dublin. Otherwise you pass under Cope Bridge and on to Louisa Bridge you will soon come to the ruins of the old staging house. The towpath along this section is good

Wild life on the canal at Cabra

for walking with firm gravel under foot all the way to Louisa Bridge. Viewing platforms erected along here give excellent views over the Rye Valley and the river below. A short distance beyond the old house a path leads down to the old spa basin.

History

The Deep Sinking (Carpenterstown)

Just beyond Granard Bridge at Carpenterstown is the start of the Deep Sinking. In 1789 before construction began, the Canal Company were strongly advised by their part-time engineer Richard Evans to avoid bringing the canal through this area. John Brownrigg, an eminent land surveyor, offered the same advice, describing the area "as a stumbling block of the most serious nature". Both pieces of advice were ignored by the directors, due to the influence of the Duke of Leinster who wanted the canal to pass by his estate at Carton. Work began on excavating through Carpenterstown Quarry in July 1791, and it was estimated that the work would cost £10,000. More experienced navvies were employed on the section. They were paid at a rate of between 1s 6d and 3s 4d per cubic yard removed from the cutting. A small plot of ground was also provided on which they could erect a small cabin to live in. Although the cutting is only 1.7mls long, it cost more

The Deep Sinking

than £40,000 to excavate, £10,000 of which was spent on tools and gunpowder. As you walk along, it is still possible to see, in places, the holes in the rock into which the gunpowder was poured for blasting.

Porterstown

A little more than half way along the deep sinking is Kennan Bridge at Porterstown. Just before you reach the bridge, watch out for the steps hewn into the side of the canal bank, leading down to a small spring well which bubbles from the rock close to the water's edge. In the days before piped water was available in the area, this well supplied the community with fresh water.

The tall unusual gothic building, on the right hand side of Kennan Bridge, was at one time Clonsilla National School. Opened in June 1853 and built at a cost of £900 it is 60 feet high and 30 feet wide. Many legends and stories abound about the school. Legend has it that the local landlord, Luke White (Lord Annaly), refused to allow the building of a Catholic school on his property. Two brothers, James and Charles Kennedy, wine merchants from Capel Street, acquired a piece of land from the Royal Canal Company and built the school. Legend also has it that the local Catholic priest put a curse on Luke White's castle, near Luttrelstown, "that a crow would never build a nest, a ewe would never lamb or a hare would never run on his estate". The school closed in 1963.

The plaque at the Deep Sink, Clonsilla

Between the bridge and the school, on the evening of the 26th of November 1845, the worst disaster in the canal's history occurred. A boat left Broadstone for Longford at 2pm with forty seven passengers and a crew of seven on board. By the time it reached Porterstown, the evening was cold, dark and wet. Just beyond the bridge, the boat struck the bank. Frantic passengers rushed to the escape door causing the boat to fill with water and it began to sink. Those lucky enough to be up the front were able to escape. Sixteen people were drowned including a Mrs. Mulligan. This lady and her young child were returning from Boston in the USA. However, the child was among those saved, but not so lucky was young Alfred Grenning who drowned on that terrible evening. Another of the passengers, Private Jessop of the 8th Hussars, who was returning to his regiment in Longford, saved many lives; while the local people helped the injured and took them back to their homes.

An inquiry into the accident revealed that when the boat passed under the bridge, the steersman passed the helm to Patrick Teeling, a young man who had boarded the boat further back along the line, where he had being carrying out repairs to the canal bank. Teeling was unable to steer the boat thus causing the accident. Many of those who died in the tragedy are buried in the Church of Saint Mary's in Clonsilla. The simple plaque on the bridge commemorates the disaster and was unveiled by members of the Royal Canal Amenity Group on the 25th November 1995.

Clonsilla (Callahan Bridge)

The suburbs of Dublin have reached out beyond the village of Clonsilla, but it still manages to retain most of its rural charm. The village and its hinterland have many places of historical interest waiting to be explored. The nearby Luttrelstown Castle was built in 1200 by Geoffrey Luttrell and the family occupied the castle for six hundred years. In 1800 it was sold to Luke White for £180,000, but since then it has had many owners, including the members of the Guinness family. Over the years it has entertained the rich and famous alike. Queen Victoria visited Luttrellstown on two occasions; an obelisk in the grounds commemorates her visit.

Saint Mary's Church, at the top of the village, was built in 1830, replacing an earlier church of 1550. The stained-glass window by the artist Evie Hone depicting Saint Fiacre was installed in 1937. Interred in the church grounds is the body of Most Rev. Patrick Fitzsimons, Archbishop of Dublin, who died in 1769. Shortly after his death it became customary for the coffins of deceased Catholics to be placed on his gravestone while prayers were recited before burial.

St. Mary's Church Clonsilla

Pakenham Bridge (Barberstown)

By 1792 the work on the canal was in total chaos. Work was underway on different sections between Dublin and Leixlip. The workmanship was so bad that many of the locks had to be demolished and rebuilt. Some of the bridges also had to be rebuilt; this bridge collapsed causing the death of four workmen.

Cope Bridge and the Rye Water Aqueduct

It's a short walk from Cope Bridge to the ruins of the old staging house. Just beyond the old house you will notice that the width of the canal narrows and the bank changes from clay to stone. You get a better view of the aqueduct from the river. The terrace of steps cut into the steep bank take you all the way down. In the days of the passenger boats, intending passengers would board the boat at this point. On cold days they would sit in the waiting room of the house, where a fire and candle light was provided. Although the house was single storey in the front, it was two storeys at the rear. Here the horses that worked this section of the canal were housed. The family who collected the fare, lit the fire, and took care of the horses, lived

in the remainder of the house. Shortly after the Royal Canal Company was formed, the Duke of Leinster had persuaded his fellow directors to re-route the canal through his village of Maynooth. This diversion necessitated the building of a large aqueduct to carry the canal over the Rye Water 100 feet below. This brought the canal nearer than planned to the town of Leixlip. The arch and the aqueduct, which carry the canal over the valley and the Rye Water, were designed by the company's engineer Richard Evans. Construction began in July 1791, but the heavy rains of that November washed the foundations away. In 1792 similar problems were encountered, which slowed the work considerably, and the aqueduct was not completed until 1796. The total cost came to £28,230 18s 5d, more than three times its original estimate.

Leixlip Spa

Just beyond the old staging house a path leads down to the Rye River (Water) and Leixlip Spa and basin. The spa was unearthed by workmen digging the canal in 1793. Newspapers of the time gave graphic descriptions of how the event happened: "it immediately issued in a narrow perpendicular stream from the bottom of the bed, to the astonishment and alarm of a labourer with whose naked leg it came in contact."

The Royal Canal Company re-routed the warm spring to the side of the aqueduct, into a shallow hexagonal shaped pond, and from here it flowed down the side of the valley to a brick basin. This was used as a bath when the spa was a popular visiting place, particularly by the poor of Dublin, on Sunday afternoons in the late 18th century.

It is recorded that on a Sunday between 6am and 5pm in August 1794, that 55 coaches, 29 post chaises, 25 noddies, 82 jaunting cars, 20 jigs, 6 open landaus, 21 common cars and 450 horsemen and a sizeable number of pedestrians visited the spa. Its popularity was such that the Rt. Hon. Thomas Connolly, on whose land the spa was discovered, intended to build a pump house and a hotel, but he died before the work could commence. The area around the spa is considered an important amenity area because of its ecological, historical and archaeological interest. The plant-life in the area consists of Watercress,

Meadowsweet, Harrow Grass, Bog Pimpernel, March Horse-tail, Butterworth and Lady's Smock. In June and July, many species of Orchids can be found and in late summer, the dangerous white-flowered Hogweed flourishes close to the river.

Leixlip

Leixlip is the easternmost town in Co. Kildare and was probably the western boundary of the Scandinavian Kingdom of Dublin in the 13th century. The town gets its name from the Old Norse *lexhlaup* meaning Salmon-Leap. Leixlip Castle, on the River Liffey, was built in the twelfth century, but the village itself dates from the medieval period. The local Church of Ireland church, St. Mary's incorporates a medieval tower.

Because the River Liffey passed through Leixlip, industry thrived in the town. In 1732 an iron works was operated by the Molyneux brothers and their partner John Twiss. In 1824 the mill was taken over by James Hill. His produce was transported to Dublin and westwards via the canal. The town also had a flour mill and a woollen mill. At this time it had a population of 900 and had seven grocers, six public houses and a shoe maker.

The windows in the Church of Our Lady's Nativity in the town were designed by the renowned stained glass artist Harry Clarke in 1925. The statue of Joan of Arc was a gift from the French Ambassador to Ireland.

The Canal near Leixlip

Leixlip Spa Basin

WALK 5

Louisa Bridge
To
Maynooth, Co. Kildare

Distance	3.6 miles (5.8km)
Terrain	Hard walking surface, with some grass

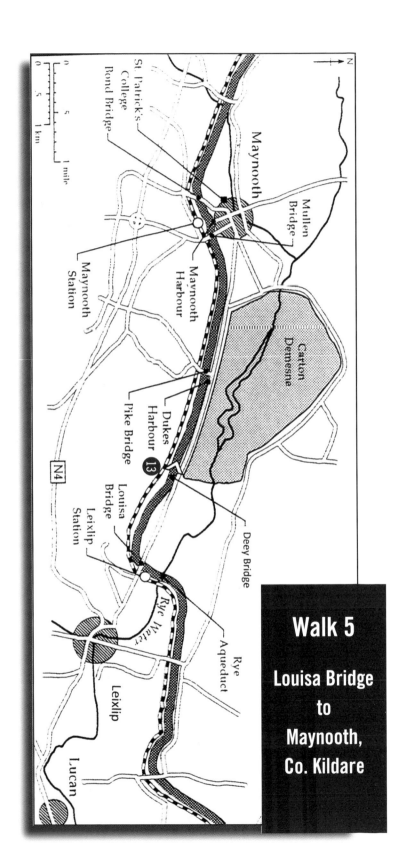

N →

0 5 1 mile
0 5 1 km

Rond Bridge
St. Patrick's College
Maynooth
Mullen Bridge
Maynooth Station
Maynooth Harbour
Carton Demesne
Dukes Harbour
Pike Bridge
13
N4
Louisa Bridge
Leixlip Station
Deey Bridge
Rye Aqueduct
Rye Water
Leixlip
Lucan

Walk 5

Louisa Bridge
to
Maynooth,
Co. Kildare

Louisa Bridge to the Harbour at Maynooth is just over 3.5 miles (5.8km). It makes an ideal afternoon's stroll allowing some extra time to explore the historic town itself. For the first half mile of this walk the new housing estates of Leixlip are visible on the far bank of the canal. In the distance to the north, the impressive Intel computer factory can be seen. A half mile beyond Louisa Bridge you encounter a new structure; (Collinstown Bridge 16A) was built over the canal in 2003. The 16A refers to the fact that it is located between the 16th and 17th bridges on the canal.

Soon after passing the new bridge the noise of the traffic fades into the distance as the canal bends away from the main Dublin to Galway road, (R148). You will rejoin it again at Deey Bridge where you cross through the narrow turnstile to the 13th Lock. This was the first lock to be restored by RCAG in 1977.

The avenue of trees and hedges that lines the canal bank ends at Dukes Harbour, just before Pike Bridge, 1.15 miles (1.8km) from Deey Bridge and 2.1 miles (3.37km) from Louisa Bridge. The Bridge spans the canal and railway almost directly opposite the entrance to Carton Estate. The high stone wall on the far side of the road surrounds the estate,

Deey Bridge 13th Lock

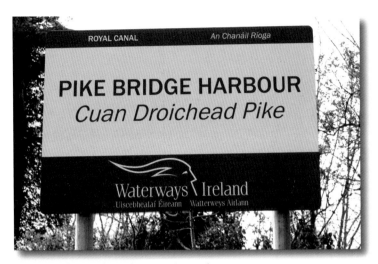

Duke's Harbour, Pike Bridge near Maynooth

home of the Dukes of Leinster. This area up to the bridge is known as" Dukes Harbour", and was built for him so as he could cruse the canal in his own boat. The all-weather surface and seating around the area it makes an ideal spot for a short stop.

As you emerge from under Pike Bridge, you get a quick glimpse of Carton House. Soon, you get your first sighting of Maynooth, when the spire of the church in St. Patrick's College appears above the trees in the distance. From Pike Bridge to Mullen Bridge is 1.35 miles (2.1km). Just beyond the bridge is Maynooth Harbour. The area is a wide expanse of water with lots of seating set into the restored stonework that surrounds it. The children's playground is a major attraction, while fishing and wild life is in plentiful supply.

Maynooth Railway Station is on the south bank of the canal. Access is from Mullen Bridge, or over the steel footbridge that spans the harbour. The canal is only a short distance from the town centre, and you will find lots to interest you. It's well worth taking the time to explore it.

History

Louisa Bridge

Louisa Bridge is the only bridge on the canal named after a woman. The lady in question was Louisa Connolly, wife of Thomas Connolly of Castletown House, who was also a Royal Canal Director. Other directors who had bridges named after them, on this section were, Robert Deey, William Pike, Joseph Mullen, and James Bond.

A little more than a mile (1.3 km) beyond Louisa Bridge is the 13th Lock. This marks the end of a 7.5 mile (13km) stretch of canal without locks, from the 12th Lock at Talbot Bridge, Blanchardstown. In the past, the 13th lock had the reputation, among old boatmen as being haunted, and they would never moor here overnight.

Carton House and Demesne

When the canal was first proposed in 1789 it was never intended that it would run through Maynooth, but much further to the north. The 3rd Duke of Leinster, a director of the canal company, had the canal rerouted through the town and past his house and Demesne at Carton.

The 13th Lock

Carton (Baile an Cairthe, town of the pillarstone) was part of the manor of Maynooth, granted to the Fitzgerald Family in 1176. The Fitzgerald's only took up residence at Carton in 1739 in a house built by the Talbots of Malahide, on land leased by Sir William Talbot from Gerald, 4th Earl of Kildare in 1603.

In January 1739, Robert Fitzgerald, 19th Earl of Kildare bought back the lease and employed the German architect Richard Cassels to remodel and extend the old house. The body of the house was lengthened and the two wings were raised from two to three storey's, with open curved colonnades connecting them. Portland stone was imported from England, and the interior was decorated and plastered by Paolo and Filippo Lafranchini. The plaster work on the dining room ceiling carried out by the brothers cost £500, a very large sum of money at that time. Robert Fitzgerald died in 1744 and the work was completed in 1747 under the supervision of his wife Lady Mary O'Brien.

Robert's Fitzgerald's son James, the 20th Earl of Kildare and first Duke of Leinster had little to do with Carton in the early days. He spent most of his time at the family townhouse in Suffolk Street, Dublin. However, James considered the house in Suffolk Street to be insufficient for a man in his position.

Entrance to Carton House

He acquired a site for a new house on Coote Lane in the Molesworth fields on what was then the unfashionable south side of Dublin. The new house was named Kildare House, and was completed in 1745. Within a few years residential development began in the area and soon Coote Lane was widened and renamed Kildare Street. In 1761 James was created Marquis of Kildare and in 1766 first Duke of Leinster, at that stage Kildare House was renamed "Leinster House".

James and his wife, Lady Emily Lennox, was largely responsible for the development of Carton Demesne. In 1766 high walls were built to enclose the 1,100 acres, and the grounds were landscaped. Trees were planted and the Rye Water, which flows through the Demesne, was widened and a lake created.

Carton House and Demesne have changed very little since the 18th century. It was one of the finest stately homes in Ireland and is of huge historical significance. The Fitzgerald family sold Carton in 1949 and in recent times it was developed as a hotel and golf course.

Maynooth

Maynooth, like many Irish towns and villages close to Dublin, has developed and expanded rapidly in recent years. The town of Maynooth has a long and distinguished history. The Fitzgerald Family were Norman sent to invade Ireland by Henry II in the second half of the twelfth century. Like many strangers to our shores, in time they became more Irish than the Irish themselves, adopting their language and customs. Their descendants became "Earls of Kildare" and later "Dukes of Leinster".

In 1176 Maurice Fitzgerald, a close associate of Strongbow, was given land in the district of Maynooth, where he built a castle. Over the following decades a small village developed close to the castle and a century later in 1286, it was granted a weekly market and an annual fair. The Fitzgeralds were one of the most powerful Norman families, almost independent of their master, the King of England. They eventually fell foul of the Tudor monarchs and the castle was besieged by an English army in 1535 and partly destroyed. It was rebuilt in 1630, but in less than twenty years it was once again in ruins when Royalist forces attacked it in 1647.

Although the town continued to have a market and fair, growth was slow. It was not until James Fitzgerald returned to live at Carton that radical changes began to take place. In Ireland, this was a period of improvement and redevelopment in many towns and villages, particularly those who had a resident landlord. The demesne at Carton was phase one of his development plan, followed by the village in 1756. The project took over forty years to complete and involved widening the main street and building several smaller ones off it. The street pattern in the town remains virtually unchanged to the present day. The 18th century Georgian houses have been retained and any new developments reflect the same design.

The canal with its fine habour had little impact on the local economy in the town. It provided a passenger link with Dublin and an access route for large quantities of coal used by St. Patrick's College.

The College developed around Stoyte house and its fifty acres of land close to the castle. It opened in 1795 as a seminary, with fifty students. Until then students studied for the priesthood on the continent. The new college reduced the number travelling abroad, where it was felt that they were influenced by revolutionary philosophies.

By 1835 the College had over five hundred students, which was reflected in the town's trade, particularly the tailoring trade. In 1824 only one tailor was recorded, but by 1846 the number had increased to six.

The famine of 1845 had little effect on Maynooth. The town was sustained by the employment provided by the college and the Duke of Leinster's estate. St. Patrick's College became a Pontifical University in 1869 and a recognised College of the National University in 1910. Lay students were admitted in 1966.

Selected Bibliography

Bath, Ian and Delany, Ruth, Guide to the Royal Canal of Ireland, Dublin , 1994.

Clarke, Peter, The Royal Canal 1789 to 1991, dissertation, Trinity College Dublin, 1991.

Clarke, Peter, The Royal Canal, The Complete Story, Dublin, 1992.

Clarke, Peter, The City Basin, Royal Canal News, Dublin, 1993.

Delany, Ruth, Ireland's Royal Canal, Dublin, 1992.

Exploring Maynooth. Five self-guide historical walks. Maynooth, 2000

Fewer, Michael, Irish Waterside Walks, Dublin, 1997.

Neary Bernard, Dublin 7, A Local History, Dublin, 1992.

Mac Thomais, Eamonn, Me Jewel and Darlin Dublin, Dublin, 1974.

Mac Thomais, Shane, Glasnevin, Ireland's Necropolis Dublin, 2010.

The Wood-Wall Walk: Clonsilla Historical Society

Between Leixlip and Maynooth

The 12th Lock, Blanchardstown